I0038982

THE TWO-FACED BROTHER

Smile of an Angel, Soul of the Devil

Marcia L. Taylor, BA

BK
ROYSTON
Publishing

BK Royston Publishing
P. O. Box 4321
Jeffersonville, IN 47131
502-802-5385
http://www.bkroystonpublishing.com
bkroystonpublishing@gmail.com

Cover Design: Elite Book Covers
Cover Photo: Lee Alexander

ISBN-13: 978-1-955063-04-3

Printed in the United States of America

Dedication

This book is dedicated to God, the head of my life, who has opened doors to make this book become a reality in an effort to help others find Christ and live healthy DV free lives.

I dedicate this book to all DV survivors and those who work tirelessly to help victims of DV escape abuse, and to those who are looking for a way of escape, but feel trapped, ashamed and feel no one would ever understand. There are women shelters in every city and counselors there to guide them and help them start over and move forward.

Acknowledgements

To Dr. Lee Alexander, who never tired of reading my scripts and giving constructive criticism.

To Charles Smith, who's always there to help. To my mother and best friend, Ivy Blair, who never got tired of listening as I read to her.

To my son Clifford A. Taylor, my Daughter Maria L. Stewart, and my grandchildren who are my inspiration and love of my life.

Table of Contents

Introduction

This book is compiled of true and fictitious stories. The names were changed to protect their identities. The fictitious name of the woman telling the story is Tamela.

Many women felt if they found a man in church, she'd be safe, and he'd be a real brother. However, there are two-faced brothers, but they all have red flags. A two-faced person is one who pretends to be your friend and then starts calling you names as soon as you leave the room. Do you know the red flags? If not, perhaps this book will help you.

Are you living with a secret of domestic violence? Why is it that so many women feel ashamed to admit they are in domestic and/or violent relationships? Domestic violence covers a wide spectrum of physical, psychological, economic, and sexual abuse. It often results in low self-esteem, isolation and possibly death. It was once thought that one in every ten women are either choked, beaten, slapped, threatened, or slammed into walls or furniture. CDC reports one in every three to four women have suffered such violence. It is not always from a partner. The violence can also come from parents or other family members.

I lived with an abuser for a short time. It nearly cost me the life of my infant son as I held him while being beaten. Although I was trying to protect myself and him, he slipped from my embrace to the fold of my arm as I kept him from falling to the pavement. I am thankful I left him and the city after some months. I was one of the blessed ones.

There are many red flags in dating relationships that women should be aware of, and men too for that matter. It was years before I attended a domestic violence class or a traumatic recovery empowerment mentor (TREM) class, to teach others and to help others realize it wasn't your fault, you are somebody, and the importance of telling someone when you are in trouble. I want to give back with this factual-fictional book to help other women who are caught up in this vicious DV cycle.

Today, I write this book in honor of so many clients I have helped to escape domestic violence. By sharing their stories and sharing techniques and identifiable red flags, I learned in classes how to help others who are still suffering and feeling alone and ashamed to get help. I write this book in an effort to avert needless years of pain and suffering.

Perhaps I've saved a life!

Family Secrets

I sat sipping tea, looking out of the window, listening to the steady pitter-patter as rain fell in a rhythm on the window seal. Two squirrels chased one another playfully from branch to branch in the big oak tree in front of our large ranch-style home. Donald had promised to have the house painted white from the current pale green but never seemed to get around to it. However, I was grateful our home was spacious, especially after growing up in a small two-bedroom apartment. All four of us always nearly bumped into one another daily. My brother, Aaron, slept on the sofa bed in the living room, which allowed my sister, Nancy, and I to have the other bedroom. Sparkle, our

2-year-old German shepherd, was a house dog. I still remember his beautiful brown silky fur with just a hint of black on this head. He was so friendly yet protective. My parents gave him away because we could no longer care for him, and there was no such thing as a food stamp allotment for dogs during that time, such as there is today.

When I was only nine, my Dad was robbed and beaten to death while standing at a bus stop while home on military leave. I still remember his beautiful hazel eyes that seemed to always be so bright and shiny with joy. He just lit up the whole room when he walked in. I loved the way he always picked each of us up to give a big kiss and a hug. He and Mom seemed to be so much in love. She was so sad and different when Dad died. She worked in the shipyards and was always tired, so Nancy and I started cooking dinner early to surprise her. Since I was the oldest, I got to pick the menu. Nancy pretty much swept and dusted and Aaron was good about keeping up the bathroom and taking out the garbage. We didn't have a lot to eat, but it was our family secret.

We had so much love we didn't really notice that we were poor. (We were raised on the theory that what happened in the house stayed in the house. You did not put your family business in the street.)

Mom usually wore one of her favorite two dresses when she wasn't wearing her work pants. She saw to it that my brother and sister and I had nice clothes for school. I hated those

Buster Brown shoes with thick soles, and I used to try and rip the heel off on the curb so I could get new shoes, but I finally gave it up. I never told Mom how much I hated those shoes; that was my secret. Saturday night was bath nights, and we kids had to share bathwater. Everyone took turns being first, but we never told a soul. That was the family secret! It was years before I learned why Dad sometimes ate last when he was home, saying he wasn't hungry yet. Those were the times we had very little food, so I guess Dad had a secret too...to make sure we had enough.

However, Nancy could never keep a secret! At dinner, we had a favorite plate with flowers on it and a favorite seat near the window. I chuckled to myself when I thought about the time we let Nancy sit in the favorite spot and eat from the favorite plate. The condition was that she not tell Mom we were outside playing ball in the street before she got home from work. Well, as we were eating, Nancy was so into her food, and putting the last bite into her mouth, and said, "I'm not going to tell mom that you guys played in the street," without thinking….it's our secret." Aaron and I froze in terror…no privileges for us as I saw Mom turn slowly from the sink. We were going to have a very warm bottom because our secret was out!

Thanksgiving

My tea grew cold as I continued to reminisce about that warm and beautiful day I sat in the Single's Group at church. I was noticing the beautiful bright colors all of the sisters wore in mid-June and I recall thinking one day I'd meet the right brother. Then my lonely days would be over. We'd take long walks holding hands, enjoy our meals together, and laughing. We'd be excited when our workday ended and raced home just to have those special moments together and share our day. I felt joy as I thought of us attending services together and praying together each night before retiring.

I smiled as I recalled how I looked across the room and saw Donald smiling at me. I looked to see if perhaps he was smiling at someone next to me, but there was no one there. I felt really warm and happy inside. Donald was very handsome; he always dressed so nice and smelled so good. He knew all the answers in Bible class, drove a nice car, sported a big ring, and rumored that he had his own home since he was 25! All of the single sisters had their hats set for him, and he knew it. My heart pounded as I gave a faint smile back. I felt weak as he headed toward me at the end of the session and ask me to coffee. Wow, I'm eight years older, and I couldn't believe he was asking me out with all of these beautiful young sisters in the singles' group. Maybe God has finally answered my prayer, I thought as I accepted and had tea.

In the days to come, Donald called me each day. Sometimes he even called me from his job at least two or three times a day to ask what I was doing or where I was and how I was. I felt so lucky that this man was thinking of me even while working! He always opened the car door for me and was polite; he pulled back my chair when dining out, ordered for me, and never tried to kiss me at the door for weeks.

Wow, I thought, what a brother! I'd had two months of bliss!

He began bringing flowers or sending flowers, and he even sent electronic cards and pictures of flowers to my email. He loved to walk holding hands as though he read my mind, and if another man looked at me, he'd quickly put his arm around my waist or shoulder to show how proud he was of me. I was so flattered! I had never met Donald's family, and he didn't speak of them much. In fact, he'd change the subject when I brought them up. He did say his mother lived in Chicago with her new husband, who he didn't seem to care much for. His father had left his mother and his two brothers when he was a small boy. He never talked about his two brothers, and he said his childhood was not a very happy one. I tried to probe once, but he became very angry, so I never revisited it again because he had become a different and ugly person. He just wasn't very pleasant when he was angry. I didn't know that was a red flag.

We continued to see one another, and I felt I was the luckiest woman in the world to have such a handsome man eight years younger and so in love with me. Well, Thanksgiving rolled around, and I invited Donald to our Thanksgiving dinner to meet my family. My daughter, Janice, and her husband, Jake, an air force pilot, flew in the day before. It was rare for him to be able to come. Donald showed up with flowers for my mother, and she was so overwhelmed she cried. Nancy and my brother in-law, Paul, and the kids drove in from California. My brother, Aaron, now a policeman in Nevada, flew in. My son, Thomas was in the service and unable to attend.

Donald stole the show! He talked on and on and was so knowledgeable about everything.

It was during the dessert time that everyone was stunned. Donald took his spoon and tapped on his glass. Everyone froze. Donald stood up and went on about how wonderful I was and how happy he was to have met such a warm and friendly family, and how he'd love to be a part of it. Then he turned to my mother and stepfather and said, "Mr. and Mrs. Johnson, I ask your permission to marry your daughter, Tamela if she will have me." He turned to me with this huge and beautiful ring and said as he knelt with tears, "Tamela, will you marry me, my darling?" My mother began to cry, my stepfather smiled and hugged my mother, my daughter, Janice laughed, and she and Nancy began to clap. Yet my brother, Aaron, and my son-in-law, Jake, just sat there with frozen faces. I'll never forget it! I was too happy to figure it out.

I said, "Yes, yes, yes, I will!"

We married on Valentine's Day because Donald didn't want to wait until next June as we had planned. We rented out my small three-bedroom home, and I moved into his lovely 4-bedroom home with a swimming pool, and it just as lovely as everyone had said. It had plush white carpet everywhere, huge and expensive pictures, and his dog fluffy was even white! We both had our own bathrooms, and believe it or not, we each had our own bedrooms, and we could meet up in the shower. It was a dream! The first few months were blissful! Sometimes he'd beat me home and have a candlelight dinner prepared. Other times, there would be a flower on the bed and candles around the tub!

We went out to dinner at least once or twice a week and then to the movies. Donald would even take me to a live concert, or bowling, long drives, and walks along the beachfront. I'd never known so much happiness! There were some things about him that I didn't understand, but I was too happy to bother about it.

For example, Donald insisted that I sleep in his room three nights a week; Monday, Wednesday, and Friday in that order. He said the absence would make our hearts grow fonder! For the first few months, Donald came to my room on Tuesdays and/or Saturdays. Still, after a while he stopped. Donald made me quit my executive position at the K and B Television

Station. He said he was fully capable of taking care of his wife. The flowers began to be further and further apart. The hugs were fewer, and he began to make excuses when it was time to visit my folks. He called from work two or three times a day, and if I visited my mother, he'd call me over there and want to say hello to Mom. We never kissed much because Donald said he didn't much like kissing. Here I thought he was being a real brother! He got so he didn't like me visiting my family much and said he wanted more of my time. Wow, what love this man has for me, I remember thinking.

Where's Donald?

I recalled our last week in Vegas before moving to Oregon. It was one of the hottest summers I'd seen in Vegas, and we both went to the store in our shorts as we often did. As I got out of the car, a man looked at me, nodded with a smile, and was about to get into his car when Donald began cursing and yelling at the man! "I saw how you looked at my wife's legs, and if I catch you looking at her legs like that again, I will take you down!" I was shocked and afraid. The man, not wanting any trouble, quickly apologized, got into his car, and drove off. When I tried to calm Donald down, he said in a loud outburst, "It's your fault, if you'd put some clothes on and stop flirting with other men,

I wouldn't have to put them in their place! I was both shocked and hurt. Who was this man I had married anyway? Where was the warm, soft spoken, loving, romantic, Bible-reading man I had married? Where's Donald? I'd never seen this jealous side.

We moved to Oregon. Donald said it was cooler, and we wouldn't need to wear shorts all summer since the ocean was nearby. He was very quiet during the next few months. We stopped going to the movies and out to dinner, and we never walked together anymore. I called mother nearly every day. Donald spent a lot of time on his computer and out on the patio on his cell phone most evenings. He began to come home so late that I often ate alone. When I asked questions, he would just say, "I have to make a living, don't I?" He always paid the bills and controlled the budget because it was his idea of taking care of a wife. I never knew how much the mortgage or insurance was, or even how much he made. I was given a fifty-dollar monthly allowance. At first, I was happy not to have to worry about bills and it didn't matter. I never went anyplace, except to get my hair done, and I didn't know anyone.

I cried so much that my mother knew something was wrong, so when Anthony, my stepfather, retired from his job, they moved to Oregon at my mother's request. They found a small home just two miles away and on the same side of town. To my surprise, Donald was irate about it. One day, I told him that I needed more money to get both my nails and hair done.

"You have a $50 a month allowance; take it out of that!" "Donald, that's not enough for both, and I need a few dollars left to spend on things I might need", I said. I couldn't believe this was the same man that had been so sweet bringing candy and flowers. "Then make a choice," he said, and he walked off. I was stunned. Who was this man? I followed him into his room, asking what had happened and why he'd changed. "Don't you love me anymore," I asked. "Did I do something wrong?" He didn't answer. He just continued taking off his shoes. I walked up to him and lifted his chin to kiss his lips.

The next thing I knew, I was flying across the room and landed on my bottom. My head hit the dresser. I sat there, stunned. Who was this monster? What had I done? I began to cry.

"That's it," I whimpered; "I'm leaving you!" He jumped up and began to hug me, crying, "I'm sorry baby, of course, I love you, I don't know what got into me! It's just job pressure. I'll make it up to you. I promise it won't happen again. Of course, I'll give you money to get your hair fixed, I want you to stay beautiful!" He gave me $50 more and begged me to stay in his room with him though it was a Tuesday.

Spiders

The next day at breakfast, I chattered on as though nothing had happened. When he got up to leave for work, he hugged me and said,

"I'm sorry I got upset with you last evening,

Tamela. You know I love you, don't you?"

"Yes," I said.

"It won't happen again," he said and left. He called later to ask how I was and if I needed anything from the store. I was shocked. In the days to come, his calls home became more frequent. Then one day, Donald came home early to find me lying on the sofa watching television. I had just cleaned the house, did the laundry, and dinner was in the oven.

Donald flew into a rage. "So, this is all you do all day while I am working my butt off to take care of you!" He began to wipe his hand over the tabletops and the fireplace mantle. Dirt, he loudly shouted, dust! I apologized and got up quickly to get a dusting cloth for the mantle, and I said, "Donald, I just dusted yesterday, but maybe I missed something."

"Shut up you slut!" I couldn't believe what I was hearing as I stood shaking. Before I could do or say anything at all, Donald slapped me so hard I nearly blacked out. I fell to the sofa, stunned and in pain. My head was spinning, and my heart pounded as though it would jump out of my chest! I began to scream from fear.

The more I screamed, the more he hit me. Finally, I went limp. I was too weak to move. There was no strength left in me to scream. I lay on the floor with tears streaming down.

The doorbell was ringing, and someone was pounding on the door. Donald said, "Get up and go to your bathroom and get yourself cleaned up, and I'd better not hear a peep from you, or you'll get more!" I limped to my bathroom, but I could hear Sue from next door asking if everything was okay. Donald chuckled, "Oh yes, Tamela is afraid of spiders." I heard Sue laugh as she left.

That night, Donald came into my room with an ice pack. "You shouldn't upset me Tamela. You know I'm under a lot of strain at work, and I am working so hard to take care of you. Don't you know I love you?" "Yes," I replied weakly." He put the ice pack on my swollen face, noting the left side was worse than the right side. Donald stayed with me and held me all night as I wept softly to myself while he slept.

I usually talked with my mother daily, but my lip was swollen, and it was too painful to talk.

So, I didn't call her for a few days, and when she called, I pretended to be busy. When other family members called, I gave the same excuse that I was baking or something, and I really felt bad to tell a lie. I had two black eyes and a swollen cut lip, and my face and shoulder hurt something awful. It would have been all-out war if my family could see my face, and my brother, Aaron, would have him arrested if he didn't beat him to a pulp first. Donald and I grew further apart, and my shoulder hurt so badly it was difficult to sleep. I begged Donald to take me to the doctor. Finally, one night it was so bad I cried and cried. When Donald saw the swelling around my shoulder bone, he became frightened and took me to the emergency room.

After x-rays, the doctor came in and told us I would need surgery, but first he'd want to speak with a specialist. The doctor put my arm in a sling. He looked at Donald with a very stern face and turned to me and said, "How did this happen, Mrs. Polman?" Donald began to explain quickly that I had fallen.

The doctor cut him off and said sternly, "I was speaking to Mrs. Polman." Donald stood quiet, but I could tell he was angry, and the look he gave me said, "You'd better not tell."

"Yes, that's right." I lied. "I fell down the basement steps with a load of laundry."

"Alright," the doctor said, "I'll get things started." Of course, Donald added smoothly that it had happened while he was at work or wouldn't have let me carry anything heavy down the stairs.

Still, the doctor wasn't impressed as I looked at his face and he began to write in my chart. He wrote out a prescription for pain as he said, "I trust there will be no more falls down the stairs." No spider on earth could bring the fear and pain this man had brought into my life! He was the spider!

The Bus Ride

A month later, I was told the tear was too bad, and the bone was separated, and it was felt that surgery was not an option at this time. I would have to learn to live with this pain during the next year. Donald stated that he needed a "whole woman," and our sex life had nearly dried up, and we had grown very far apart. He seldom came into my room, nor did I visit his room. We ate in cold silence. He'd sit with the newspaper in front of him to avoid looking at me, and I sat starring down at my plate most of the time. I never got up to walk him to the door anymore, and he just kissed my forehead and said, "have a nice day." Nevertheless, Donald never failed to call home at least three times a day to see if I was home or what I was doing. I felt like I was in a glass jailhouse looking out!

Sometimes he'd call and say I won't be home for dinner. When he did come home in the middle of the night, I could smell perfume on him that wasn't mine. I cried a lot.

It was a hot July day when Nancy and the kids were here for a week visiting my mother. She called and said the kids wanted to ride on the max, which was something new and like a mini train. So, they picked me up, and we parked in the park n ride area and were having a great time going down memory lane. Her four-year-old had changed seats to sit next to her six-year-old sister, Margaret. Five minutes later, a middle-aged man sat in the seat she'd vacated.

Jamie got up and waddled up to the gentleman and pointed her little finger in his face, and said, "you need to get up because I was sitting there first!" Everyone began to laugh. The man asked how old she was. "Four," my sister replied blushing and apologizing.

He laughed and said, "Wow, she is really bright. She's fine, no worries." Conversation ensued. I learned this man worked with abused women as a counselor. He gave me his card as he was about to get off and said, "If you know anyone in trouble, have them give me a call; I can help." He smiled and got off the max. Why me? 'Could he tell,' I thought. Could Nancy tell?

We had a wonderful day. Nancy treated me to a new hairdo at a salon at the mall; the kids rode on the merry go round and enjoyed ice cream. We had a wonderful lunch, but I was worried about being gone all day and missing Donald's calls. I hoped he wouldn't be angry. Nancy looked at me over lunch and said, "Sis, is there something bothering you, is there something you'd like to talk about. You look nervous."

"Oh no, I'm fine, just tired." We laughed about the bus ride and Mr. Blackburn and headed home.

When I got home, Donald wasn't there. What a relief. I quickly put together a meal, although I knew the chances were very slim he would come home on time to eat. I knew there had better be dinner on the stove just the same. I went to bed early still pondering over the man on the bus ride.

During the next few years, Donald had slapped me around so much that I couldn't hide it anymore. I finally told my mother, and she was furious but said something had bothered her about him over the last few years and she'd noticed how withdrawn I was. She hugged me, and I wept softly in my mother's arms. Mother wanted to call the police and have me press charges before my brother, Aaron, or my son, Thomas noticed my change. Thomas was now home from the service. He missed the Thanksgiving dinner and proposal and even my wedding to Donald. When he did finally meet him, he never liked Donald. I couldn't bring myself to press charges. I decided to stay with Mom and Dad for a few weeks. During those weeks, Donald constantly phoned begging for forgiveness. He sent flowers to both my mother and me. Dad refused to allow me to speak to him on the phone. When he showed up at church, I wouldn't look at him and always rushed to the car with my parents before he could get near me.

One day Pastor Edwards phoned me and requested I come in and talk with him. When I arrived, Donald was there. I turned to run to the car, but I heard Donald yelling, "I'm sorry; I'll make it up to you! I've repented and just need you to listen!" I stopped and went into the office with them. The Pastor talked about forgiveness.

He said he would work with us once a week, and so on while also going through scriptures. He spoke to Donald about treating the wife as the weaker vessel and to love his wife as Christ loves the church. I moved back to our home that night. My mother cried, and my Dad was livid!

The next few months were heaven at best! It was just like the beginning of our marriage. We visited Mom, but it was always a thickness in the room, and the conversations were forced. When Donald was at home, he was his old happy self again. Love notes were pinned on the refrigerator, candles around the bathtub, and frequent visits to my bedroom at night. I just had to remember not to upset him when he came home tired, I thought. Slowly the new Donald began to arise. He began giving me $50 a month again and asking me how I spent each dime. I never realized that this financial abuse and was a part of domestic violence. The money that was allotted to me each month was slowly taken away from me. I had no money for my hair, which was my only outing lately, nor for my personals. Donald said we needed to put our money together to pay the bills, so my $50 allowance was put aside for a while for emergencies. When he did give me $50, it came with a brutal night of sex. I assumed he was keeping $50 a month for himself, but I was afraid to ask. I know now anger is a DV control tool.

I recalled when I decided to ask him how much his allowance was, He flew into a rage. I'd never seen him like this, not even the day he hit me.

"Are you questioning me?" he charged.
"After all, I do for you! I work hard to give you the best, to put food on the table, I buy your clothes, and you have a nice car to drive!" Yep, he sure did, I thought. Donald picked out clothes mostly fashioned for older women! I could drive the car only when he said I could! I tuned back in to hear him saying, "Now you don't trust me? What is it, you don't want me to have anything like my friends?"

I kept apologizing for upsetting him and told him it wasn't important and to just calm down. I ran into my room crying. I heard him calling me a cry baby and ranting and walking back and forth like a lion. I was so frightened, wondering if he would come into the room and hit me again. He didn't, but I wondered I hadn't realized how much fear and anxiety he had created. The relationship was magical at first, gifts, attention, constant calls, telling me constantly how beautiful I was. Then the blaming began and I was always saying, 'I'm sorry' and walking on eggshells, so to speak. The sudden change and decrease in affection and attention once I showed how much I cared for him was a red flag I didn't catch. It left me feeling confused, depressed, I was full of self-doubt and shame. When he noticed it, he would just turn up the charm again, so I married him. It was time to move on at that point in a hurry. I realized I needed help, but who could I turn to? I began to think about the man on the bus ride again.

I'M NOT CRAZY!

Over the next few weeks, I noticed many phone calls that only rang once and then stopped. Donald would disappear for hours at a time, claiming to be working at the office. At least it was peaceful. I knew not to question or make him angry. When I told the Pastor during one of our sessions, Donald explained it all away by saying he'd raise my allowance, so he had to put in more hours. It was my fault! I knew not to dispute him.

We stopped at the grocery store on the way home, and I was driving because Donald claimed he wasn't feeling up to driving and insisted that I drive. When we came out of the store, I didn't see the car. "Oh my God, Donald, the car is stolen," I blurted. "We must call the police!" It was then that Donald spotted it two rows over. "But I didn't park it there," I exclaimed." "Well, it didn't park itself!" Donald retorted. Was I losing my mind? Surely Donald wouldn't repark the car. He did have keys.

Over the next few weeks, I could hardly locate my cell phone. It was just never where I recalled leaving it. I began to wonder if I had early onset of Alzheimer's disease. Whenever we were at my parents' home for dinner, Donald never failed to bring it up. He'd tell my family that I was getting worse and how patient he tried to be with me, but Nancy didn't buy it.

She said under her breath one day while eating dessert, "Why do you stay with him? "Don't stay until he drives you, crazy sis."

I choked up and quickly played it off by saying, "Oh, he's okay; he's better." Then one day, I was coming down the hall to ask Donald if he was ready for dinner when I caught Donald moving my purse and keys to another spot. I smiled to myself, "I'm not crazy!"

Little did I know this was also a form of domestic violence and mental cruelty. All this time, I thought I was losing my mind from the stress I was under, and Donald was having fun.

'This man was the crazy one,' I thought. I'm not crazy after all!   Be aware, people, be aware!

THE MARKET

Nancy and the girls had gone. I had felt kind of blue the last few weeks. I cleaned the house twice a day, checked for dust on the mantle, under pictures, and everywhere I could think. I watched television until I felt like throwing it, I was so bored. It was a dreary, rainy day, but I decided to go to the market to get fish and fresh vegetables. Donald loved fish, and it was Friday. Whoever started this fish on Fridays anyway, I thought. While looking at the vegetables, I heard my name from behind. When I turned around, I saw it was none other than Mr. Blackburn, the counselor from the bus ride. "Why hello, what a surprise," I gasped.

He'd remembered my name. We made small talk, and he brought up support groups again and invited me to the next session the following week. I don't think I need that, I lied. "I'm happily married." "Well, there are pointers that will help keep it that way, and perhaps you have a friend that is not as lucky as you are and may need our support," he said.

"That may be," I said. I told him that I would think about it. Still, I wondered if he could tell how miserable I really was.

Mr. Blackburn had the brightest personality, and his smile seemed to make his whole face just glow. On the drive home, I battled myself within, thinking it couldn't hurt to go and help fill my lonely days. Maybe it was meant for me to go to the market.

TREM

I'd been attending the support group classes for several weeks now, and I found myself looking forward to them. I learned that the meetings were really called TREM, and it stood for Traumatic Recovery and Empowerment Meeting. I wasn't sure if it was because I enjoyed staying behind to help clean from the snacks or the rides home from Mr. Blackburn when I couldn't use the car. It bothered me sometimes when he looked into my eyes because it was as though he was looking right through me and knew my dark secret. I knew I was getting closer to confessing my dark secret of pain. I pretended I was there to help someone else suffering.

I had learned so much. I learned most abusers came from a long history of domestic violence in their homes. Many have unaddressed anger and domestic violence issues. They range from psychological, verbal, physical, economic, sexual, spiritual, and collateral where children are involved. Moreover, there were two sadistic cases involving animals. It was during one of those cases that I threw up right in class.

Cedric told his story of being forced to have sex with his dog after his father and then being violated by his father monthly for 6 years. I cried. It was then that I realized women are not the only victims! Cynthia had sex with her dog while her husband watched then he beat her for being bad. She'd run away, but her husband always found her until he finally died from a heart attack.

So many women are in the denial state. They blame themselves, and it was wonderful to see how Mr. Blackburn drew each of us out of our state of mind to realize it wasn't our fault. Each woman also realized she was wonderfully and beautifully made by God and important with many talents. I came to realize that anger is a tag or symptom of abuse or control.

As a matter of fact, there are many red flags to alert individuals to the characteristics of an abuser. For example, low self-worth, poor communication skills, poor impulse control, and mean tempers. Abusers seem to have a need to control, tend to drink, smoke marijuana, or do other drugs, blame their partner for nearly everything, usually have low self-esteem, and brag about what they can do. They enjoy rough sex feel that beating their mate makes them a better person, and they don't allow anyone to question them.

Mack told of how his wife always cursed and belittled him and hit him with pots and pans because he wouldn't fight her. She didn't drink or smoke, went to church, wore long dresses, but was meaner than heck. He told of how the children walked around cowardly, and when he came to their rescue from her yelling and swatting them across their small faces, she'd take it out on him. At one time, this is who he thought was his dream woman. They finally lost the children, and he moved away. We never saw Mack again after that session. Sometimes

I think it must have been painful for him since there were so many women talking about the male abuser. Mr. Blackburn then began another class on a different night, which was just for men. We began role playing to learn how to recognize abusers and how to respond. Oh, how I began to live for those support group sessions. I wasn't crazy, and I surely wasn't alone!

BED OF FIRE!

Over the next few months, I learned to open up and share bits and pieces of my marriage. I made new friends, and Donald was so busy staying out late and doing his own thing that he hardly noticed me anymore. He sometimes took both keys to the car to keep me locked in the house, but I always caught a ride, or Mr. Blackburn would bring me home if I had no ride. I was careful to look for Donald's car before getting out of his car.

One afternoon in class, I listened quietly as Mary Belle told her story, pausing to weep briefly at intervals. She told us how loving and sensitive Timothy, her husband, seemed at first. She had known him since childhood, but circumstances separated them for a number of years. Later they met again at a party. He always wanted to hold hands in public once their relationship grew. He would call her at least three times a day from his job to check on her and say sweet things. She stated that out of nowhere he began to be short tempered and would go into a rage over small things. For example, if the toothpaste was being squeezed in the wrong place, the bread tie was twisted the wrong way, or the kids playing ever so softly that even got on his nerves while he studied to be an engineer.

Timothy had already flunked the state exam twice. He blamed her stating she didn't keep the kids quiet. She cried as she told us how the slaps changed to strikes in the face with his fist. And how he'd pick the kids up by the neck to bring them up to his face to yell and curse them for little things. She said he stood 6 feet two and was heavy. She told of how Timothy's mother beat him and his siblings with a belt, then locked them in a dark closet. He was angry because his father had another woman and another family living only a mile away.

She told how he began accusing her of seeing someone out of the clear blue sky and sometimes choked her at night as though trying to choke the truth out of her. At one point, she wept almost uncontrollably when she told of being raped by one of his friends. Then he kept her awake all night to retell her story over and over again. He didn't believe her. She said she finally had a nervous breakdown and spent two months in a psychiatric ward learning that it was not her fault. When she was released, he had filed for a divorce. He took the children and was seeing one of her childhood friends. Timothy later married the woman and moved her into their home. We all gave her a group hug and reminded her that it was not her fault and that she had been a good mother and wife. Mr. Blackburn told her that she was beautiful inside and out and not to let anyone tell her different.

After that one, we all needed a break. I couldn't help but think that in all of my suffering, I was still blessed. Before I knew it, Mr. Blackburn was calling us to attention and said we had time for only one more account that could be shared. Joneese begin her story of how she had waited for her husband, George, to come home from the service for 10 years. She said the first three weeks were bliss, and she had never known such happiness. He would come home with flowers or cook special meals for her and served her dinner with wine.

Soon, she realized he was drinking more and more wine and larger amounts and that his personality was beginning to change. He began to accuse and tell her that his friends told him she had been a real slut while he was in the service. He began taking pills along with the wine to calm him down, which worsened things. Joneese broke down uncontrollably for a few moments as she described her brain aneurysm resulting from George beating her head into the cement until she was unconscious. After which, he forced her to have sex with him while she was in excruciating pain. She told of the headaches that led her to drink excessively and become dependent on pills.

When she finally got up the nerve to tell him she was going to leave, he grabbed her purse, took all of her identification, medical cards, and credit cards. Then he severely beat her and bashed her head into the wall. Blood was everywhere. Her aunt came out of her bedroom with a hammer raised and said, "I'm going to get you!" The kids were screaming. He jumped up from on top of her and ran out of the door. An ambulance took her to the hospital for stitches. Several weeks later, he began calling and crying and begging forgiveness and asking her to take him back. He said he was in counseling and was all over drinking.

Yep! She took him back. They went to church together, he quoted scriptures, and everyone just loved him. Several months went by, and slowly he stopped going to church, saying he was tired. Then she began to smell alcohol on his breath at night, and his eyes were glassy. He became irritated, and soon began slapping her. She warned, "If you don't stop, I'm leaving you, and I'm taking the kids with me." He apologized, tucked her into bed, kissed her, and turned out the lights. Joneese fell asleep only to be awakened by the smell of smoke. Her bed was ablaze! He had set the bed on fire and was just sitting there watching. He told her she could never leave him, or he'd burn her and the children alive! He then forced himself upon her with sick sex after helping her put everything out and getting the kids back to sleep.

Joneese said it took her months to finally get the nerve to run to a police station with her children and tell the police. She and the children were placed in a shelter out of town. George was arrested, and she and the children moved from Ohio to Oregon. An advocate told her about the TREM classes, and here she is.

After she stopped crying, she said, "I am so glad I have come. I didn't think I could ever tell anyone what I have been through. I now know that George was not the same person I knew many years ago and that it wasn't anything I was doing wrong. He needs help that he should have gotten long ago. I now know I can work and take care of my children, I'm not alone and I can make it on my own!"

We all clapped as she sat beaming.

THE KEPT WIFE

Several months passed, and we actually had homework! We all told why we were in the class and the positive steps we made since participating. Then we had a surprise guest.

Wilma said hello and congratulated everyone present, for taking charge of their own lives and began to talk about her story. Mr. Blackburn had introduced her to the class stating that she had graduated from a previous trauma class in Nebraska. She now heads up her own trauma class called TWOM (Trauma Warriors on the Move) in another city.

I noted how something about her seemed to make her taller than 5'3". She stood with shoulders back, and took charge with her manner and powerful voice. Her golden-brown hair with gray streaks around the edges flowed gently about her face. I tuned back in as I heard her say, "I was a kept wife."

She told of how her former husband, Jay found her attractive, so much so that he called her his beautiful jewel. He was so loving, affectionate, polite, romantic, and, best of all, attended church! He just swept her off her feet. However, later she learned she was just his shelf trophy. He pulled her from the shelf when he needed to show her off at work functions, family, and friend gatherings, and then completely ignored her at home. He was rude with hateful, sadistic words that seemed to flow so easily when they were alone. He spent little time at home and seldom ate a meal with her.

Finally, he was gone for weeks at a time. He never drank, but she suspected drugs, though she never saw any. What about his job? She stated that she was very lonely and began to wonder what she'd done wrong to turn him against her. She stopped fixing herself up, except when she knew he was coming or if he was home, though he always bought her beautiful clothing to show her off. It was on one of those long two-week trips that he returned accusing her of seeing someone. He had the locks changed and replaced them with deadbolts that took a key to get in and out of the house. The only difference was he never stayed away more than a night after that. However, she noticed a man sitting in a parked car in front of the house on the nights her husband was away.

A few months later, he brought in a woman, he called Crystal, that he stated had no place to go and was just a friend. "She can stay in the guest room for a few months," he roared. I didn't have a choice, as he had already slapped me once and gave me a black eye when I stood up to him. I was heartbroken. A strange woman with skimpy clothing on and hard makeup was to stay in my home without me having any say so. He locked us both in. She sat around chewing and popping gum and watching tv all day. She never cooked, and not that I would ever trust it, and never cleaned up behind herself. We ate together in silence except for occasional small talk.

"I noticed Crystal and my husband seemed to have long and quiet conversations in the living room while I did the dishes. Once I told him it would be nice if she'd come and help with the dishes, but he said she was our guest. They stayed up later and later after I went to bed. Then one night around 3 a m, I was awakened by heavy breathing and sounds coming from the guest bedroom. I jumped out of bed and ran down the hall to the guest bedroom and opened the door. The scene sickened her as he lay on top of Crystal."

"Don't you ever knock," he said as Crystal laughed. She ran back to her bedroom crying and packing. He followed her.

"Just where do you think you're going?" he roared, "Put all of that "s" back," he yelled standing there naked. "Get used to it! This is my house! I pay the bills, and I say what goes on here!"

"The next few weeks were almost more than I could bear," she stated. "I could hardly eat or sleep. My husband was sometimes in my room and other times in her room. Finally, he brought home a tall, heavy man named Carl.

My husband said the guy was a friend of Crystal's who would be staying for a few days. That very night, Carl came in our bedroom and begin to undress in front of me. I screamed for my husband, but he never came. This man, Carl, raped me at least three times before daybreak. I showered and slumped down to the shower floor crying and scrubbing over and over and still feeling dirty when I finished."

"I locked the door, but Jay just burst right through it and cursed me out and told me to get dressed and fix breakfast. I did. The next few days were very hard. Then one day Jay received a call, he and Carl took off running for the car saying they'd be right back. They yelled for Crystal to follow, but she was in the bathroom and they couldn't wait. I grabbed a few things and took off too. I never looked back. I heard that all three were arrested for drugs and sex trafficking, but I didn't investigate. I was an only child and never knew my parents, so there was no one to call. I was just glad I'd had enough sense to hide money in a safe deposit box!"

"I had enough for plane fare and a hotel room for three weeks in a quiet, inexpensive part of town until I found work in a fast-food place in Montana. I eventually moved to Nebraska, and you know the rest. I continued my education while working. Now my life's work is helping women who, like I, were or are victims of domestic violence, which comes in many forms. It is important for each of you to know that none of the abuse you received is your fault. Still, you must learn to be alert to the red flags in a relationship but do not take old baggage into new relationships, or you'll face failure. I am happily married now to a wonderful Real Estate Broker, and we have two teenage boys. I'll be hanging around after class to speak with anyone of you individually, with Mr. Blackburn's permission, to answer personal questions."

With that, she thanked us for listening and coming to TREM classes and took a seat at the front of the class. I marveled at how polished she was and how self-confident she was. You'd never know she'd been through so much. I want to be as strong as she is when I complete this class, I thought to myself.

Just as strong as that "Kept Wife."

THE DARK AND PAINFUL DAYS

The more I thought about Wilma, the more I kept thinking I should do something about my situation. I slept very little. I begin to lose so much weight that Donald began to complain. "I don't want any scarecrow walking around here! You should eat, or they'll think I'm starving you!" he retorted one day.

The next few weeks were very dark and painful for me. I kept wondering if I could make it on my own if I left Donald. I didn't want to worry my parents; Afterall I'm an adult, right?

I cried myself to sleep many nights, feeling lonely and helpless. What was I good for? Why was I going through this? I'm a good person. My days were very dark, and the pain was almost more than I could bear. I sat looking out of the window about a month later. It was beautiful! I saw young people holding hands, squirrels, playing in the trees, mothers pushing the infants out for a walk, and men walking their dogs. Everyone seemed so happy. Here I sat, bored, sore from beatings. I was looking old and feeling depressed and nothing to look forward to but more of the same. I lived for the class just to be around other people and to enjoy the warm smile Mr. Blackburn always gave me when I'd enter the class. He sometimes asked if I were okay or if there was anything he could do? I didn't even know what he could do!! Sometimes I left the class feeling very low to hear of women going through what I was going through and some even worst!

Then, just like that....I jumped up and started packing everything necessary; grabbed my purse and keys and drove over to my parents' home. I knocked so hard that both my parents came to the door with alarmed looks on their faces.

"What on earth has happened? asked my mother. "I've had enough! I just left Donald! Mom, Dad, can I stay here with you; just for a little while....until I find work!!"

"Of course," they both retorted gleefully. Donald called again and again, but I never took not one of his calls. I went home with my brother to get the last of what I wanted from the home while Donald was at work one day and was happy to leave him everything else. When Mr. Blackburn learned what had happened, he congratulated me, and when he hugged me, I nearly melted. That same week, Mr. Blackburn spoke to one of the professors at a nearby college. When I went in for an interview, I was hired immediately as a receptionist! I filed for my divorce, which Donald never contested.

Mr. Blackburn began to ask me out for coffee and tea or dinner. He made me laugh.

When I felt a need to talk about the past, he'd just sit quietly looking deep into my eyes giving support. He always seemed to find the right words to make me feel stronger and better about myself. I finally asked him why he gave me his card, and he stated that he had noticed a bruise on my neck and left arm and that it seemed hard for me to look him in the eye.

As time went on, after Mr. Blackburn knew I was comfortable enough, he would allow me to share with newcomers about how I felt when I first came in. I told of how I avoided telling anyone the truth about my abuse and how I blamed myself, thinking I must be doing something to make him hate me. I shared how much I had grown by taking the classes until one day I found the courage to make the change, but that was something I had to do. I had to be the one to walk away from those dark and painful days.

WHAT DID I LEARN?

It is impossible to share all that I learned. Still, I am excited to share some of the main red flags on behalf of those who are domestic violence survivors. Sharing helps others prevent the agony and pain many of us have suffered. I didn't realize when I first joined the group that keeping secrets from them was a prime example of avoidance of the truth. The fact that I had been abused and controlled was placing me in greater danger of facing further abuse, a lack of help, skills, and knowledge to recognize the red flags at the onset.

Abusers may use the blaming defense for the abuse saying, "she made me mad," or they blame alcohol for their behavior. "I flunked my test because she didn't keep the kids quiet while I studied." The abuser may have grown up watching this behavior or were abused themselves, which is their "norm." The red flag of anger is a husband being beating and shut in a closet, so he grew up with hidden rage. Now in a relationship, he has frequent anger outbursts. They will minimize their behavior by saying, "she likes it because she still wants to stay with me." A red flag is when they bring you flowers and call you constantly and say things like, "I like you because you are not like the "lazy winch" I used to date who thought she was Queen Mary." Or he may call her crazy or a whinner. If he speaks of his last date like that "RUN."

When I had to account for every dime and could hardly obtain enough money for my personal needs, this was a type of financial domestic violence. Belittling me and moving the car and/or car keys and pretending I did those things and forgot, was mental abuse. That too is a part of domestic violence. So, when a man buys a coat, jewelry, or anything else and you can only wear it with him, and he takes it back, this is a red flag. He has real control issues that will only heighten if you continue the relationship. He may offer to help you with your budget, and then you find him taking liberties, like the use of your car or credit card without permission. Other things include doing things to interfere with your job, borrowing money and not paying it back, and always making excuses or saying things like "I thought you loved me."

Be careful of the religious deceivers who have deceived himself! He may be a Bible quoting man who continuously speaks of the scriptures and talks about government and everyone else is less than Godly than himself.

He could need meds or have a severe underlying psychological issue that is very dangerous. He may have been abused by a religious fanatic and is off balance by the silent pain he is suffering. One woman told of many things she suffered because as a young child she had to get up at a specific time and do the can-can dance in her grandmother's basement during some time of religious service and was defecated on all over a boy. She's getting help since she told her story, but what about him? A religious red flag is when he tries to isolate you from those who believe as you do. He may refuse to attend services with you, belittles your beliefs, and may even try to influence your children. He may have other odd behaviors, such as washing his car daily. Believe me, I've heard or seen it all. Many women are so busy falling in love that they forget about the safety of their children. A sexual red flag is when your new friend loves to sit your child on his lap, or the overly friendly gym teacher or touchy music teacher gives free lessons. Tag along to all your child's lessons.

JOY

Over the next few years, I learned there are still good, respectable men who are also looking for a loving and respectable mate. They are just waiting for a Christian woman who leaves all baggage behind and is ready to receive love. She must realize that she must first love herself, love God, forgive those who have hurt her in the past, and know that she deserves a loving man of God. It all begins with friendship. With each week that passes, Mr. Blackburn and I grow closer together with respect. Both of us enjoy the genuine feeling of real friendship.

We laugh together and talk about our families, school, politics, religion, goals, and dreams. He met my family, and I met his. We even had joint dinners where we all seem to be one happy family. We discovered that we both would love to live in Canada. We also love to eat fish and chicken, kale and collard greens and rhubarb pie. He doesn't like peanut butter pie, and I don't like pumpkin pie; therefore, we have both at our functions. We enjoy walking the waterfront downtown, holding hands, sitting on the park benches while eating sandwiches, and feeding the birds. He's a camera bug, and I wait patiently as he snaps away, and the finished products are always just breathtaking. I love the way he holds my hands when sitting across from me and looking so deeply into my eyes with those very bright hazel brown eyes. It's as though he looks right through me reading my thoughts, and then he always says such beautiful things, but there are times that he just looks, and those warm eyes seem to speak volumes.

He listens so patiently when I need to talk about all that I have been through then speaks just the right words into my spirit. I find that he loves me with a healing love, and never passing judgment. Once he said, "It wasn't the man, but a wicked spirit he allowed to invade his body." You must not hate or give him power over your life. He then prayed for me, and I felt a peace come over me and a weight lifted. I never even knew he was such a devoted Christian because he never wore it on his sleeve. I learned that he was brought up in church, taught Sunday School, and was the church counselor. Wow, what Joy! I had hit the jackpot!

Then one day, sitting in a small diner, I said, "I hope Donald finds happiness because, for the first time in my life, I feel pity for him and a freedom I have never felt before."

He said, "Thanks to God you are a strong, beautiful survivor and you deserve love. I love you dearly."

It was at that moment he looked deeply into my eyes and said, "I love you so much that I hope one day to make you my wife!" I was so overcome with happiness that I cried with joy.

He knelt down and with a beautiful ring said, "Will you marry me and make me the happiest man in the world?"

Of course, my answer was a big YES! I had finally found a real BROTHER! We were married six months later. It was a June wedding just like I'd always wanted. I went back to school, and now we team teach TREM classes and enjoy helping others put their lives back together who are "DV Warriors!"

www.ingramcontent.com/pod-product-compliance
Lightning Source LLC
Chambersburg PA
CBHW072208270326
41930CB00011B/2578